HOW HIGH IS UP?

Mark J. Beasley

Illustrations by

Kem Welch

ISBN: 979-8-9910778-1-1

Illustrated by Kem Welch
Produced by Publish Pros | www.publishpros.com

Acknowledgments

Kem Welch for continuing his entertaining and creative expertise in illustration, adding a visual captivation at the turn of every page.

Laura Schwarz for her aid and assistance throughout the entire writing process of revising and polishing the work.

Erika Nein for her advice in editing my manuscript.

Rich Carnahan for his organization, vision, and his overall guidance in the publishing of this book.

Contents

How High Is Up?

How high is up
In this world of ours—
Taller than buildings,
Higher than towers?

Taller than trees,
Higher than wire—
Certainly, up
Must be a lot higher?

Over the top
Of a mountain's peak?
How do we measure—
What's the technique?

How far does it reach,
When we look to the sky?
Do airplanes and birds
Even fly that high?

How far does it go?
Forever perhaps.
How do we know
If there aren't any maps?

Does up reach as high
As the eye can see?
Or could it be more—
How high could it be?

There's no way to tell,
There's no way to know.
There's no one to show us
How high it can go.

Up is way up there—
Pretty high, I suppose,
But what we don't know,
Is how high it goes.

Permanent Nomad

There's a band of nomads
Who will not travel.
And if ever they did,
Their world would unravel.

They're somewhat motionless,
And it's very effective.
A stationary lifestyle's
Their primary objective.

You'll never find them
Roaming the land.
You'll never find
Their tracks in the sand.

They'll pile in a Chevy,
Turn off the ignition,
Lower the anchor,
And hold their position.

They don't need maps
To plot their course,
They don't need mules
Or even a horse.

They'll stay put,
Wherever they are.
They'll get rid of the tires
And live in their car.

These people don't wander.
These people don't roam.
These nomads consider
Anywhere, home.

They're standing their ground.
They're not going away.
Pretty strange for some nomads,
Wouldn't you say?

Be Clever Whenever

It's cool to be smart—
It's cool to be clever.
It's cooler than cool
To be clever whenever.

It's not ever clever
To be pointless, you see,
To never be clever
As clever can be.

So be not the fool—
Rather, be always clever.
It's cooler than cool
To be clever whenever.

Salem

In the founding days of Massachusetts
The people lived in fear,
Back in 1692
Or around about that year.

Wicked witches used to ride
Old broomsticks through the sky,
And spooked the people of Salem town
And the villages nearby.

Once the night crept in upon them,
The villagers were quick to find,
Those mischievous wicked witches
Were not too far behind.

They'd be swooping in on broomsticks
And hurling incantations,
Casting spells and sorcery
In various locations.

But what if they had vacuum cleaners
To ride on through the sky?
And what if they had electric power
And receptacles nearby?

Then the people of Salem town
And all the villages therein,
Would've been in a different situation
Than the situation they were in.

Imagine witches on vacuum cleaners
Instead of broomsticks when they flew.
They're fortunate there was no electricity
Back in 1692.

The Mountainside

They had to carve a tunnel
Through the mountainside,
To open a path from east to west
And conquer the Great Divide.

They cleared the entire passage,
Moving tons of rock and ore.
They're not going around the mountain
Like they did the day before.

Then they laid the railroad track
With mallets, spikes, and sweat.
Engineering a unique design
That no one would forget.

When they finished this master plan
And swept away the gravel,
They opened up the tunnel
For everyone to travel.

All the people were astonished
At this engineering feat,
And the government was satisfied
That the project was complete.

Soon came all the masses,
To colonize the West.
First, they came sporadically,
Then came all the rest.

They all established settlements
From the mountains to the shore,
And all those people lived their lives
Where they never lived before.

Thus became the USA,
Spreading far and wide—
All because they carved a tunnel
Through the mountainside.

Timmy Never Learned

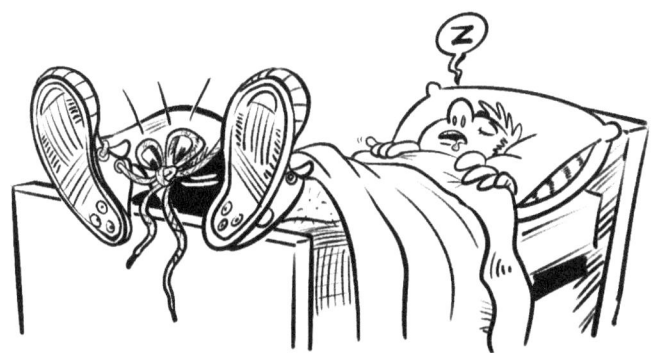

Timmy couldn't tie his shoes,
Because Timmy never learned.
This was some astounding news,
And his mother grew concerned.

This was something new to Timmy—
Territory uncharted.
Because every time he tried to tie,
He gave up before he started.

"Tie your shoes," said Timmy's mother.
"Tie them good and tight."
"Tie your shoes," said Timmy's mother.
"Tie the left and right."

"You must learn to tie them
On your own," she told her son.
"You must learn to tie them
Without help from anyone."

He took his sneakers left and right
And thought a moment in his head.
He tied his sneakers good and tight—
Like his mother said.

They ended up both tied together
The first time Timmy tried.
And Timmy grew secure in knowing
That his shoes were finally tied.

Timmy crawled into bed that night
And quietly settled in,
Knowing he never needed any help
To tie his shoes again.

The Crop Duster

This is the task
Of the crop-dusting man,
Dusting off crops
As fast as he can.

And when the sun is rising,
And daylight is revealed
It is not surprising
To see him in the field.

Every ear of corn
And every row of wheat
Is dusted off completely
Until the dusting is complete.

He dusts off the barley
Where it happens to grow—
Stalk after stalk
And row after row.

Soy by the acre,
And every tiny bean
Is uncontrollably dusted
Until it's perfectly clean.

And he won't stop
Until he's absolutely sure
That every single crop
Is absolutely pure.

There is no duster
Of crops better than
The non-adjusting,
Dust-busting,
Crop-dusting man.

Who Is Who?

No matter who you are—
If you're famous or you're not;
If your bank account
Has little money
Or maybe has a lot;

If you're the first one born
Or the second or the third;
If your babblings border genius
Or they border the absurd;

No matter how you look,
No matter what you wear;
The way you walk,
The way you talk—
I don't even care!

If you are you
And I am me
And they are they
And we are we,
And everyone identifies
With whom they ought to be,

Then I'll be me
And you'll be you—
That's what it's all about.
I think we've got this
Who is who thing
Finally figured out.

Teeter-Totter

I climbed upon a seesaw
Directly after school.
I did not follow instructions.
I did not obey the rule.

I tried to teeter-totter,
But I didn't bring a friend.
I really needed someone there
To sit on the other end.

With no one on the other side
To balance out the weight,
I couldn't get momentum,
Nor could I levitate.

It's hard to teeter-totter
When you're sitting there alone—
Like a one-way conversation
When you're talking on the phone.

Although my end was on the ground
I can also verify,
That the other end was simultaneously
Pointing to the sky.

Gravitation, my undoing,
Inertia was to blame.
The effort didn't matter much—
Results were all the same.

After half an hour
I'd had about enough.
You see, the going down was easy,
But the going up was tough!

Dinosaurs Are Forbidden

Dinosaurs are forbidden
In my neighborhood.
This rule's non-negotiable,
And it's well understood.

The fine is enormous
If a dinosaur is found—
It's illegal to have
Any dinosaurs around.

So I dressed my dinosaur
In a clever disguise,
To fool the inspector
Should suspicion arise.

I measured him thoroughly
Because my intention
Is avoiding detection
And unwanted attention.

I fashioned a suit
From his head to his toes,
And I kept it a secret
So nobody knows.

In a regular crowd
He blends so well,
That if anyone sees him
They couldn't tell.

In form-fitting trousers,
Two shoes on his feet,
A pair of socks
Made it nearly complete.

I fastened a necktie
At the base of his throat,
Then topped it all off
With a long overcoat.

The tailor-made outfit
Is the perfect attire.
What else could a dinosaur
Ever desire?

He's cleverly disguised
So he won't draw attention.
He should fit right in
With no apprehension.

The disguise works perfectly—
Like I hoped it would—
Because dinosaurs are forbidden
In my neighborhood.

Hands Off the Chocolate

Don't eat the chocolate,
Have the sorbet.
Don't even think
About chocolate today!

Eat apples or oranges
Or bananas or beans,
Broccoli or bacon
Or a can of sardines.

Have something healthy,
Have something nutritious.
Have something satisfying,
Have something delicious.

Why not something
That grows on trees,
Or comes from the ground,
Like carrots and peas?

You can have candy,
Or you can have cake.
You can have sausage,
Or you can have steak.

Have something edible
That you can chew.
But hands off the chocolate;
It's not for you!

Mr. Harris

Mr. Harris starts out every morning
Right before the dawn,
Out there in his front yard,
Attending to his lawn.

He starts off with the scissors
And a ruler and his gloves,
Down there on his hands and knees,
Doing what he loves.

Which, of course, is cutting grass
As anyone can see.
Quite frankly,
I don't think there's anywhere
That he would rather be.

Measuring every single blade
To the proper elevation,
Until he feels he's truly made
An accurate calibration.

And with a systematic snip
He moves on to another,
And cuts a perfect carbon copy,
Exactly like the other.

Crawling along, inch by inch,
Measuring blade by blade,
Clipping every single one
Until every cut is made.

You might think it's overkill.
You might say he's irrational.
But his grass is neater
Than the putting greens
At Augusta National.

And I watch him
From across the street
Until daylight's finally gone,
Fascinated by the peculiar way
Mr. Harris cuts his lawn.

An Excellent Statue

A man's been standing
In the ancient square,
And for quite a long time
He's been right there.

He's been giving off
This spellbinding glare,
Which captivates onlookers
Who stop and stare.

And then they leave
The ancient square,
But that man continues
To stay right there.

He hasn't moved a muscle.
He hasn't budged an inch.
Maybe it's rigor mortis
That has him in a pinch.

Perhaps he's simply nervous
With everybody staring.
Maybe he's not comfortable
In those silly clothes he's wearing.

I've never seen him blink,
And I've never watched him twitch.
I've never seen him scratch,
If he's ever had an itch.

I've never seen him wiggle,
And I've never seen him squirm.
I've never heard him giggle,
I can honestly confirm.

But he always draws attention
As he captivates the mob.
This guy would make
An excellent statue
If he ever needs a job.

Boiling Water

The one thing that proves difficult
For this modern generation
Is bringing water to a boil
For a cooking situation.

If you want to boil a pot of water
And you want to boil it now,
Follow the guidelines listed here
And I will show you how.

Do not take a shortcut,
Do not veer from these directions.
Follow the instructions step-by-step,
And do not skip any sections.

This method has been tested,
And this method never fails.
So imitate this method,
And comply with all details.

First, you fill an empty pot
With water to the top.
If it begins to overflow,
That's when you need to stop.

And when you have the right amount
Of water in the pot,
Just heat it on the burner
Until it's boiling hot.

Then remove the boiling water
From the burner's heating coil.
Now you see why it's so difficult,
Bringing water to a boil.

Trade-In

Bought myself my very first car
Right off the production line,
Way back in 1928—
No, I think it was '29.

I really admired the fancy machine
And its new-fangled body design.
I paid the man hundreds of dollars,
And the automobile was mine.

"Enjoy your car," the salesman said
As I drove off the parking lot.
And I was elated all the way home
About the great deal that I got.

Now here it is, ninety years later
And trouble is starting already.
This thing is weaving all over the place,
And I can't seem to hold it steady.

The engine was spitting out black exhaust,
Which caused the car to stall.
So I had it towed to the nearest garage
To get a complete overhaul.

They did everything they could possibly do
But couldn't get it to run.
Guess I'll trade it for a 1930
Or maybe a '31.

Brainstorm

Instead of writing Santa Claus
Like I do every year,
I called him on the telephone
And held it to my ear.

I informed him of my Christmas list.
Of course, he checked it twice,
Reviewing what I ordered
Against his merchandise.

"You'll have it on the twenty-fifth,"
He said, "Delivery guaranteed.
But call me back on the twenty-fourth
If there's anything else you need."

And with that, my order
was on the way
And it happened
all because,
I picked up
the telephone
And called up Santa Claus.

HOW'D HE GET THIS NUMBER?

Plain Old Bread

I fed Ed a piece of bread,
And he ate it without any spread.
"I like it plain instead," said Ed.
"It pleases the taste buds in my head."

"Try the spread," I said to Ed,
"On yet a different piece of bread.
You'll find the taste buds in your head
Delighted by the flavored spread."

But Ed insisted that the spread
Not be spread upon the bread.
"Keep your spread," to me, he said.
"I like to eat it plain instead."

Laughing Lou

Laughing Lou, laughing Lou
Laughed at anything, it's true.
And no one ever really knew
What was humorous
To laughing Lou.

He laughed at things
That weren't even funny,
Like bumping your head
Or losing your money.

Some terrible news
That made people cry
Made Lou start laughing,
And no one knew why.

He laughed all day
So clear and loud,
You could hear Lou laughing
In a noisy crowd.

He laughed at anyone
Who tripped and fell;
He snickered at kids
Who weren't feeling well.

He giggled at people
With the tenacious flu—
It was all too funny
To laughing Lou.

Then he laughed so hard,
He lost his voice.
He had to stop laughing
Because he had no choice.

And the people had a party
And a jamboree.
The news about Lou
Was even on TV.

And from that day on
His voice was gone,
No laughing could he do.
His laughing days were surely through,
The laughing days of laughing Lou.

For anyone ever that ever he knew
Lou always laughed at them.
And since his days of laughing are through
Now they're all laughing at him.

HA HA HA!

Anyone's Guess

I tried counting stars
Only minutes ago,
How many I tallied
I don't really know.

The sky grew dark
And I laid down flat,
But I lost the count
Not long after that.

First it was easy
And I counted to three,
But I never knew
How hard it could be.

Confused I became
At the task of it all,
Like how many bricks
Do I see in a wall?

Or how many fish
Can I count in a tank?
Or how many coins
Do they keep at the bank?

Large numbers indeed
An abundant supply,
But not even close
To the stars in the sky.

Their numbers, you see,
Were ever so many—
Way more than three,
If there were any.

And they all look the same
If you stare long enough,
At planets and moons
And stars and stuff.

I counted three
And I tallied no less,
But how many are up there
Is anyone's guess.

EVEN WE
DON'T KNOW!

Silly Putty

We had no computers
What else could we do?
So we passed the time
With a handful of goo.

Putty, they called it,
For that which it does.
And silly because
Of how silly it was.

The ultimate toy,
A timeless invention.
Yet simple enough
To get your attention.

You could squash it flat
Or ball it up tight,
It was only Silly Putty
So that made it all right.

You could bind it or bend it
Or twist it or twirl it.
You could extend it
Or coil it or curl it.

You could pull it or tug it
Or pound it or smash it.
Do this and more,
But you couldn't trash it.

You could pinch it or squinch it,
Stretch it every which way—
The things you could accomplish
With a handful of clay.

You could play with the stuff
And never grow weary,
For hours on end
Well, that was the theory.

Back in those days
We didn't feel so nutty,
Killing our time
With a handful of putty.

So we passed the time
With a handful of goo.
We had no computers
What else could we do?

Crocodile in the Nile

I'm a giant crocodile,
And this is where I roam.
I'm one of many just like me
Who call this place their home.

I can hold my breath for over an hour.
I slide on the thickest mud.
I swim along the river Nile.
I sun in the gookiest crud.

I lurk beneath the murky water.
I creep along the bank.
And I remain
At the top of the chain—
Mother Nature is to thank.

I survived over millions of years
Where the dinosaur did not,
Throughout the coldest climate,
Throughout the hottest hot.

I can bite the hide
And get inside
The toughest beast I know.
There's not a place
Or occupied space
That I'm afraid to go.

I credit this to superior genes
And to fundamental skill.
I capture prey by any means,
And I guess I always will.

I swim the perilous river Nile
Along the straits and bends,
From where the river starts
To where the river ends.

Sometimes the hippopotamus
Will join us for the day.
Crocodiles don't really care for them,
But they swim here anyway.

Elephants, too, come stomping through
Splashing water on their skin.
They don't wait for invitations.
They just barge right in.

But people usually get nervous
Swimming in the Nile.
They really don't know what they're missing
Swimming with a crocodile.

So put it on your bucket list
When you're out here on safari.
And I can almost guarantee
That you will not be sorry.

There's plenty of room for everyone.
There's nothing further to discuss.
Now go put on your bathing suit,
And swim along with us.

Once Upon a Time

This watch is obsolete.
This watch is past its prime.
It used to be state-of-the-art
Once upon a time.

Now it's not worth fixing.
It's not practical to wear.
Now it's past its service life
And well beyond repair.

This watch was at its pinnacle
Not so long ago.
Now it doesn't function anymore,
But even so ...

I'm not gonna scrap it
Or throw it away.
It still tells the right time
Two times a day.

Altogether Separated

I'm a nail
And I never fail
At joining up the wood.
They knock me in
Again and again
And I hold on pretty good.

I fasten homes together,
My grip is tight and strong.
Despite the wild
And windy weather,
I stay where I belong.

But those blows upon my head
Can affect my tiny brain.
I get groggy
And the world gets foggy
And my noggin throbs in pain.

The work is good and steady,
And I just got a raise.
But I'm battered and bruised
Because nails are used
In oh so many ways.

I'm used in the kitchen,
I'm used down the hall.
I'm used in the ceiling,
I'm used in the wall.

I always follow the blueprint
As directly indicated,
So the houses don't become
Altogether separated.

But the hammer is special
To the construction crew.
Nobody would dare
Tell him what to do.

He's crafted of iron
And genuine steel.
He knows the procedure,
And he knows the deal.

He is endowed
By his own creator,
So the hammer strikes first
And asks questions later.

You will find
That I don't mind
Staying in one location.
But can't you see
That I'd rather be
The hammer in this situation?

A Mountain of Cash

Bandits robbed the bank today
With pistols and ammunition.
They withdrew a lot of money,
And they didn't have permission.

But the crooks slipped up—
They left a few clues!
Then the media blabbed it
On the six o'clock news.

They captured the thieves
And threw them in jail.
And the judge told the bailiff
That they couldn't post bail.

Had they only known
About the government's stash
With a much bigger vault
And a lot more cash.

Then perhaps they would've used
An alternative plan,
Rather than a mask
And a getaway van.

If it were up to me,
I'd guarantee success:
I'd forget about the bank
And hit the IRS.

Out Go the Lights

I went bowling
In Jeffersonville,
In a bowling alley
Up on Jefferson Hill.

I looked down the alley,
I lined up the shot,
Targeted the pins,
For the perfect spot.

And right at the time
I was rolling the ball,
A weird thing happened
In the middle of it all.

Everybody in the alley
Started scrambling about
Because all of a sudden,
The lights went out!

Bowling balls were rolling
All over the place.
No sense of order—
Not even a trace.

Patrons and people
Running into each other.
Children stood crying
And calling their mother.

Young men scrambled
In complete disarray.
Some ladies could barely
Get out of the way.

Grandfathers were battered,
Bewildered and bruised;
Grandmothers—befuddled,
And clearly confused.

Tables and chairs
Were knocked to the floor,
In a great stampede
To get to the door.

The National Guard
Had to finally intervene.
What a night of commotion,
What a chaotic scene!

And it all transpired
In Jeffersonville.
This is what happens
When you don't pay the bill.

My Father the Barber

My father is my barber
And he makes up the rules.
He uses worn-out instruments
And prehistoric tools.

There's no appointment necessary,
No regulations he must follow.
His nonchalant procedure
Is kind of hard for me to swallow.

Without delay or hesitation
I'm ushered to the chair,
Staring at the apparatus
That'll soon destroy my hair.

He whacked a little off the ears,
Choppity-choppity-chop.
Then he took the pruning shears
And started on the top.

He massacred my sideburns
And after he was done,
Butchered the back with an implement
From 1831.

My bangs looked just like brambles,
He neutralized the nape.
He left my hair in shambles,
And my head's in terrible shape.

My hair is perfect as it is
And there's plenty of it there,
But there's not a lot left over
Once my father cuts my hair.

Don't Kick a Monster

If ever you thought about
Something to do,
When there's plenty of time
And opportunity too;

When there's no one around
Demanding attention,
When simple conversation
Is not your intention;

When boredom consumes you
Turn after turn,
And there's nothing to teach
And nothing to learn;

Then do something different,
Do something extreme.
Try to do something
To let off some steam.

Do something exciting,
Do something bizarre.
Do something crazy
Wherever you are.

But whatever you do
Heed my advice,
Don't kick a monster
Because it isn't nice.

There is no benefit
To this operation,
For it causes nothing
But total frustration.

The reason behind it
Is difficult to swallow,
Nor would it be
The best procedure to follow.

It goes against logic
To do such a thing.
Who knows the results
This maneuver would bring?

He could be bewildered,
And he might be surprised.
So kicking a monster
Would be ill-advised.

This is the soundest
Advice I can give,
So don't kick a monster
As long as you live.

Better the Devil You Know

When contemplating a decision
I often seem to find,
I am somewhat undecided
When making up my mind.

The eventual looks assuring
And promising ... although,
The past can be appealing,
So better the devil you know.

And here I stand
Right in the middle
Steady and holding fast—
One foot practically in the future,
The other one stuck in the past.

One of Those Days

Ever been stuck in traffic before,

Ever had one of those days?

With cars so near

You can't even steer

Or navigate through the maze?

Everyone else is in your way

And nobody seems to care.

And you want to go

But it isn't so,

And you're just idling there.

You're poking along in the lowest gear

Because it's all that you can do.

You want to indict

Somebody outright,

But there's nobody here to sue.

It's bumper-to-bumper everywhere
As far as the eye can see.
But you're stuck on the road
In static mode,
And there's somewhere you've got to be.

Sitting in traffic the entire way
In the smoke and the smog and the haze.
And all you can say
About what you survey
Is, "This will be one of those days."

No Purpose, Plan, or Goal

My goldfish swims around all day
With no purpose, plan, or goal—
There inside the fish tank,
There inside his bowl.

He's compelled to endless cycles
Of circling around the tank.
He has designers to be grateful for
And engineers to thank.

And a modest change of scenery
Has long been overdue,
But he can't alter the situation
So there's nothing he can do.

He simply spends the entire day
There inside his bowl,
Swimming around in circles
With no purpose, plan, or goal.

Adding Machine

I think you should buy me
An adding machine—
Just look at my homework,
You'll see what I mean.

A simple equation
Causes panic disorder.
So, go on the internet
And put in an order.

My homework routine
Can drive me berserk,
But an adding machine
Could make it all work.

My system of counting
Is old and outdated,
And using my head
Makes it too complicated.

These numbers don't fit
Whenever I do it,
And I'm having some trouble
Trying to get through it.

If simple addition
Causes this kind of reaction,
Imagine what would happen
If I tackled subtraction!

This Is How It Goes

Up here, where it's freezing cold,
Up near the Arctic zone—
Where everyone goes about their business,
Out in the great unknown.

I bring these families what they need
To make it through the year,
So listen up because you won't believe
What you're about to hear.

I've got a ton of ice for sale
That I brought in from the border.
Citizens of Alaska get in line,
Step up and place your order.

The ice is cold, now you've been told:
Buy the bucket or buy the pail.
Gather 'round young and old,
There's lots of ice for sale.

Get it before it melts away,
Before there is no more.
You'll need a lot more ice this year
Than you did the year before.

And the price for ice is reasonable,
And the price for ice is right.
Enjoy the benefits ice can bring
Every single night.

Perhaps you've never considered
How ice could change your lives.
Wives can buy some for their husbands
And husbands for their wives.

It's the perfect time to buy some,
You won't find a lower price.
But I can't seem to peddle
A single cube of ice.

Not even one simple transaction,
Not one single sale.
This is how you flop in business—
This is how you fail.

No one said I'd be successful at this,
And nobody guaranteed it.
This is what I get trying to sell ice
To people who don't even need it.

Tic-Tac-Toe

In the simple game of tic-tac-toe,
There stands an X, there stands an O,
And all you have to do to win,
Is get your letters in a row.

Strategy helps a little,
So you have to try your best.
This is not some type of exam,
This is not some kind of test.

It's basic in its application,
Place your letters in succession.
You won't be judged by anyone,
This is not a paid profession.

Align your letters up and down,
Or align them left to right.
You might not win the first time,
But then again, you might.

Or place your letters diagonally,
You can win either way.
Triumph will be yours eventually,
It depends on how you play.

It's best to have a strategy
Before the game begins.
Then you simply keep on playing
Until somebody wins.

That's about it.
That's all there is to it.
Get a pencil and paper,
And sit down and do it.

Three in a row is all you need,
It's all you have to do.
But do it before your opponent
Can do the same to you.

Lots of Things Annoy Me

Hanging on the wall
Right before my eyes,
A crooked painting suspended there,
Not a big surprise.

Dangling there before me
And for anyone to see,
A crooked painting lingering
Not how the thing should be.

It's not the best work of art,
Although someday it may be.
But I only notice the crooked part,
And that's the only thing I see.

Lots of things annoy me
But mainly most of all,
Is a crooked painting on display
Hanging on the wall.

As the End Draws Near

The oldest man in the world
Is a hundred and seventy-five.
He's feeble and brittle,
He wobbles a little,
And he's lucky to be alive.

He's too blind to see who's coming,
Too deaf to hear who calls.
The future looks bleak
Because he's much too weak
To get to his feet if he falls.

He's worn out completely,
And he's going downhill fast.
His frustration shows
And nobody knows
How long he can last.

But he keeps on going,
Ignoring fatigue,
Even as the end draws near
By playing in the National Football League
Twenty-one weeks a year.

Island Conquest

A mighty army dwelt on an island.
But not too far in the distance
Stood another island fortress
In its very own existence.

Now these two armies
Were busy watching
Every move the other made,
Noting each and every weakness
For an up-and-coming raid.

Each devised a simple plan
To ensure an easy win,
And waited for the perfect time
And the battle to begin.

They crossed at night In the calmest waters
To keep their ships from sinking,
All the while having no idea
What the other one was thinking.

The sea was filled with fleets of ships
And armies quietly rowing,
And passed each other in the night
Without either of them knowing.

They rushed upon each other's island
As the sun began to rise,
But found abandoned fortresses
Much to their surprise.

They raised their flags in triumph
With victory well in hand,
As the armies took complete control
Of the other army's land.

Both the mighty armies knew
They'd frightened the other away,
And there they live on each other's island
To this very day.

The Saltwater Sea

Add salt to this,
Add salt to that.
Add salt to meat,
Add salt to fat.

Add salt to enhance,
Add salt to taste.
Add a little salt
So it doesn't go to waste.

Add it to flavor
A handful of fries,
Or sprinkle your eggs
For a tasty surprise.

Add it to beef
And sensations will soar,
You're free to add salt
Where you didn't before.

Add it to everything
When you get the notion,
Salt goes with everything—
Well, maybe not the ocean.

There's plenty of salt
In the deep blue sea.
If you've tasted the ocean,
You'd have to agree.

You can add salt
To all kinds of stuff,
But the saltwater sea
Is salty enough.

There's Always Something

Thirty-thousand feet
Is incredibly high,
Inside this airplane
Up in the sky.

I'm up here for lessons—
My first introductions.
I'm here for some basic
Skydiving instructions.

At first, I was nervous
But now that I'm here,
I have discovered
There's nothing to fear.

It's a long way down,
But I'm prepped and I'm ready.
My objective is evident,
My focus is steady.

I leap from the plane—
No stopping me now.
I hope I remember
The instructions somehow.

I'm picking up tempo,
I'm picking up steam.
This goes from one
To another extreme.

I seem to be falling
Much faster than sound.
I seem to be heading
Straight for the ground!

And something's not right.
I've forgotten my chute.
This isn't funny,
And this isn't cute.

I'm close to the ground
And I understand,
That parachutes make it
Much safer to land.

If only I remembered
To bring it along.
There's always something
That's bound to go wrong.

And if only the sky
Wasn't up so high,
And if only I had
My chute nearby.

If there were some method
To perhaps fly away,
Or if only gravitation
Wasn't working today.

If only I was falling
A little bit slower,
If only the ground
Was a little bit lower.

I'm About to Fall Asleep

I'm about to fall asleep,
The hour's overdue.
I believe I'm dozing off,
And there's nothing I can do.

My lids are growing heavy
From the gravity effect.
I'll be of use to no one
In a moment, I suspect.

I'm now condemned to counting sheep
For anyone can see,
That I'm about to fall asleep,
And that's how it has to be.

Beef Stew

I have a little trouble
When I cook beef stew,
And I can't seem to figure out
What I'm supposed to do.

It never turns out
Like beef stew should.
When I follow the directions,
It's never any good.

The potatoes never cook,
The carrots always burn,
And it never seems to me
That I'm ever gonna learn.

The corn is never pleasing
And hardly appetizing.
If the onions ever tasted good,
That would be surprising.

The peas are green and chewy
And the beef is overdone,
I don't have the nerve to serve
This meal to anyone.

All you do is take some food
And cook it in a pot.
You'd think by now
That I'd know how
But, actually, I do not.

Yes, I have a little trouble
And you know I always do,
But it only seems to happen
When I cook beef stew.

If You're Over Forty

If you're over twenty,
There's no need to worry.
So no need to hustle,
Or be in a hurry.

No need to ponder
Over what to get done.
Spend all your money,
Go have some fun.

If you're over thirty,
You don't need to care.
No plans for the future,
No need to prepare.

Cash in your pocket—
The late-night scene.
You've been acting like,
You're still nineteen.

But if you're over forty,
Then everything changes.
Everything revises
And then rearranges.

You pick up the pace,
You kick it in gear.
Retirement is drawing
Ever so near.

The pressure is growing
Every single day.
To contribute more funding
To your 401(k).

But it's not that easy,
You'll learn in the end,
To make more money
Than you're likely to spend.

So you work more hours
And you get less sleep,
Because the IRS
Takes more than you keep.

You earn what you must,
While you still can.
This is the recipe,
This is the plan.

You can't slow down,
You can't take breaks.
You have to correct
Those early mistakes.

If you're over twenty,
Then you shouldn't care.
But if you're over forty,
I can't help you there.

Hoarding Is Rewarding

Hoarders keep their prized possessions
Mainly to themselves.
They keep things in the basement
And stacked upon the shelves.

They hold on to their bounty
With a most tenacious grip.
They never drop it from their fingers,
And they never let it slip.

They clutch their compensation,
And they do not let it go.
It's embedded in their DNA
From many years ago.

And they won't share with anyone
The things that they possess.
They never peddle anything,
And they give out even less.

They don't divide their valuables
With anyone they know.
They keep their prized possessions
And do not let them go.

On very few occasions
And only now and then,
They throw away their trash
To simply hoard again.

As greedy as they really are
With riches great and small,
I can't believe they'd throw away
Anything at all.

Quicksand Castle

If you build yourself a castle
From a bucket full of sand,
And sculpt a perfect garrison
With a true and steady hand,

If you follow simple guidelines
And a meticulous routine,
You can build a sturdy castle
Like no one's ever seen.

You can build a moat around it,
It's easy to install.
You don't need to follow patterns
Or any shape at all.

The diagram is up to you
And your imagination,
Or you can always look it up
If you need more information.

But build one out of quicksand
And you'll have trouble brewing,
So before you start, you better know
Exactly what you're doing.

Nothing Hurts More

Nothing hurts more
Than stubbing your toe.
I just stubbed mine,
So I ought to know.

Your pace subsides
And your momentum slows,
If you wind up stubbing
One of your toes.

You'll cuss and you'll swear
And your toe will turn blue,
If the bone in your toe
Is broken in two.

If it aches too much,
Use ice to obtain
A numbing effect
On the swelling and pain.

And don't wander around,
You might trip and fall.
Don't hobble or waddle
Or tiptoe or crawl.

If you think it hurt once
In some agonizing way,
Imagine if you stubbed it
Twice in one day!

Mistaken Identity

As I awoke from my nap
A duck was on my head.
I said, "Why are you standing there?"
He looked at me and said:
"I realize now, we're both mistaken.
It's obvious instead,
I'm a vulture, not a duck,
And you're not really dead."

Slowpoke Sam

Slowpoke Sam was never known
For swimming very fast.
He liked competition
But his routine position
Was usually the very last.

Slowpoke Sam wanted to swim,
But swimming was hard to master.
Although he was slow
And he knew it was so,
He never got any faster.

Coaches trained him one on one
To help achieve his dream,
But he lacked the speed
That he would need
To keep up with the team.

Then Sam met a shark at the beach one day
When he swam too far from shore,
And would finally master
And swim a lot faster
Than he ever swam before.

Nowhere to Be

Here you are
With nowhere to be,
As you gaze at something
With nothing to see.

You stand and stare,
Contemplating the scene,
While looking at nothing
Do you know what I mean?

And while you're staring
Nothing is seen,
Nothing beside you
And nothing between.

But you keep on looking
And try to make sense.
This odd situation
Is growing intense.

And then you listen
For nothing to hear,
There's no indication
And it ain't too clear.

So you turn your ear
Toward the ground,
But you don't hear
The slightest sound.

And then you rise
And stand there thinking,
Two eyes peering,
Eyelids blinking.

And so you debate
On what you should do,
But you haven't the foggiest—
You haven't a clue.

And as you gaze
At nothing to see,
Well there you are
With nowhere to be.

Mixed-up Pete

This is the world
Of mixed-up Pete,
Walks on his hands
Not on his feet.

He gets where he's going
On the palms of his hands,
And the reason behind it
Only Pete understands.

Everyday tasks
Are done with his feet,
In the mixed-up world
Of mixed-up Pete.

He lands on his hands
And not on his toes,
And why Pete does it
He only knows.

To raise his hands,
He uses his feet
And nobody does this—
Nobody but Pete.

He kicks with his hands.
With his feet, he throws.
He eats with his feet,
And drinks with his toes.

His mother tries to show him
How to walk upright,
But Pete never can
Ever quite get it right.

And Pete never listens
To his father's commands.
He keeps on walking
On the palms of his hands.

Pete is more peculiar
Than anybody will admit.
No matter what you say to him,
He's never gonna quit.

And nobody knows
Why he walks this way.
But if you try and change him,
You're wasting the day.

Because he walks on his hands
And not on his feet,
This is the world
Of mixed-up Pete.

Coffee Break

If I could take a coffee break,
I'd take the break for heaven's sake,
For it's a break I need to take
So I can try to stay awake.

Make no mistake, I need a break!
It's a break that I need to take,
And if I could actually take a break,
That would be the break I'd take.

So I won't take a coffee break.
I won't make that dumb mistake,
I'll take my break
When it's time to take
Until that time, no coffee break.

The Money Tree

If only there were money trees
Growing in my yard,
Then the life I've come to know
Wouldn't be so hard.

If I ever needed some extra cash
Because nothing here is free,
I could simply step outside
And pluck it from the tree.

Imagine the excitement,
Comprehend the thrills,
Of plucking all the cash you want
In fifty-dollar bills.

So I buried fifty dollars
In the fertile soil below,
Soaked it with some water,
So the money tree would grow.

And before the day was over,
I planted fifty-dollar bills
All throughout the valley
And up along the hills.

These trees will be blooming
Later on this year,
And I'll be right here waiting
For the money to appear.

I'm hoping that my fortune
Will finally turn around,
Though it is a bit unnerving
Burying money in the ground.

I can manage being rich,
I can comprehend the thrills,
But I'm completely broke
From planting fifty-dollar bills.

Your Finest Hour

Wanna know how to do it?
Wanna know how it's done?
Wanna make a sandwich
That's second to none?

Take a piece of bread,
First one and then two—
Only the tastiest
Of slices will do.

Now add bologna,
As much as you dare—
Open the fridge,
You'll find some in there.

Between the slices
You'll place the meat,
No need for perfection
No call to be neat.

Close the bread
With the meat inside,
Some like it cold
But I like it fried.

That's about as tempting
As a sandwich can be,
So grab a napkin
And follow me.

It doesn't get better
Than bologna and bread,
It's there for the taking—
Now go right ahead.

Nothing else matters
At all anymore.
Don't take any calls,
Don't answer the door.

And make it fast,
This will not wait—
Sit down at the table,
Step up to the plate.

Your finest hour
Is finally at hand,
Your bologna experience
Is proceeding as planned.

You must be courageous,
You must follow through.
There's a bologna sandwich
That's waiting for you.

Water vs. Stone

Water comes swiftly,
Water comes calling,
Until gravity demands
Its eventual falling.

Cascading liquid
In a furious tumble
Pounds upon stone
In a deafening rumble.

Repetitive rhythm,
A bellowing voice,
Battering the rock,
Which has no choice.

Echoing drums
Of liquid intrusion
Splash upon stone
In raging confusion.

The flow then perishes
Simple and free,
Coating the landscape
In the vapor's debris.

The boulder itself
A formidable foe,
Is never a match
For the constant flow.

The stone surrenders
After years of abuse,
For the water itself
Offers no truce.

And given the centuries
Of unchanging course,
The mightiest bedrock
Succumbs to the force.

The settling water
Displaying no feature
Forms into some sort
Of serpentine creature.

It carves its own path,
It creates a direction,
It winds through the scenery,
It makes no correction.

Then it proceeds
Down an unchartered maze,
For longer than time
Can add up the days.

The destination unknowing
As it keeps on flowing,
With no earthly idea
Of where it is going.

These are the rules
Laid down by the fall,
For the water itself
Obeys nothing at all.

Watching TV

How long can we go
Without watching TV?
How long could we stand it?
How long would it be?

How long could we go
Without hearing it blare?
Could we even stand it?
How much could we bear?

Could our eyes comprehend
A desolate screen?
How would we watch it
If it couldn't be seen?

Would our ears get suspicious
If we can't hear a word?
How would we listen
If it couldn't be heard?

Would our minds wander off
From where they should be,
If we couldn't focus
On watching TV?

How would we manage
Our lives anymore?
How would we do it
Like we did it before?

We couldn't imagine
How life would be,
Without being able
To watch TV.

Now That I'm Grown

Time was abundant
As it could be back then,
So I used it all up
Again and again.

It was always present
It was always there,
More than I needed
And plenty to spare.

An endless supply
That I never preserved,
I was given more time
Than I ever deserved.

There was plenty to waste
When I was a kid,
I had all I wanted
So that's what I did.

The future approaching
But all the while,
I used it before
It went out of style.

And I squandered plenty
Through the whole affair,
And saved very little
So there's little to spare.

The amount that remains
Is incredibly small,
If there's any left over,
It ain't much at all.

Only now do I realize
I was simply confused,
And wasted more time
Than I ever used.

I couldn't recognize
That long ago,
How this would affect me
And now that I know,

It's too late to act
Or change it now.
How I wish I had saved
But a little somehow.

I did not conceive
What I should've known,
But it's all too clear to me
Now that I'm grown.

There's less than before—
No argument there—
And some time remains,
But I don't know where.

And whatever lingers
Won't last very long,
It's the same cliché—
It's the same old song.

As of now there's a little
To use up again,
But I don't have as much
As I did back then.

Were It Not for the Moon

Were it not for the moon
Where on Earth would we be,
Adrift in the vacuum
Of space, you and me?

Floating out there,
Destination unknown,
Out in the hollow
Of space all alone?

Out in a sea
Of planets and stars,
Drifting by Saturn
And Venus and Mars?

Lucky for us
We're safe and we're sound,
Because the moon is out there
Circling around.

For without the moon,
We could not survive.
We count on the moon
To keep us alive.

A gray piece of matter,
Floating in space,
Surrounding our planet
And revolving in place.

A dependable force
That governs the tide,
From top to bottom
From side to side.

To some it inspires,
To some it does not,
Nevertheless,
We respect it a lot.

It's a mere formation
With an unknown core,
Or perhaps it's something
A little bit more.

We're drifting in space
And anyone can see,
Were it not for the moon
Where on Earth would we be?

Obviously Invisible

He's obviously invisible
As anyone can see,
From the top of his head
To below the knee.

How does one locate
A man you can't view,
And he knows you can't see him
But he can see you?

Is he still in here,
Or did he already go?
He could still be near,
But how would you know?

I don't notice him,
And neither do you.
How do you find someone
You can see straight through?

You can't detect him,
And neither can I.
We couldn't spot him
With the sharpest eye.

We'll never find him,
It's evident to me.
We'll never find somebody
That we can't even see.

He's obviously invisible,
It's clearly apparent,
That we'll never locate
Anybody transparent.

There's no use looking,
Take it from me—
Invisible people
Are hard to see!

It's Always Funny

It's always funny
When humor's directed
At someone not ready
For the unexpected.

When things are going
As well as they can,
And then it doesn't go
According to plan.

It's always amusing
Watching somebody slip.
It can be hilarious
Watching somebody trip.

It can be funny
When they're sliding on frost,
And they lose stability
And their balance is lost.

Wake up in the morning
And off to the races,
Then out of the blue—
They fall on their faces!

We sometimes snicker
Watching somebody stumble.
We laugh even harder
If they take a tumble.

It's hilarious to witness,
This much is true.
But it ain't too funny
When it happens to you!

There We Were

There we were,
Lying on the ground—
Me and my best friend
Were loafing around.

Lying there lingering,
Under a tree,
No where particular
We wanted to be.

Not much to discuss,
Not much to say.
Not much to do,
Not much today.

Both of us there,
Beneath the shade.
Both of us figured
We had it made.

We didn't have homework,
We weren't doing chores,
Soaking in the essence
Of the great outdoors.

And there we were,
Lying on the ground—
Me and my best friend,
Just loafing around.

Off-Key

I told you before
About singing off-key,
But you wouldn't listen
To someone like me.

You kept on singing
In spite of the warning,
All through the night
And into the morning.

Now open your ears
And hear my plea,
And refrain yourself
From singing off-key.

Sea Serpent

There's a sea serpent lurking
That you cannot see,
And he's hiding in the water
Underneath the sea.

He swims throughout the deep,
Searching for his prey,
And his victims think they might
But they won't get away.

His fangs are like needles,
His claws are like knives,
And everything that sees him
Swims for their lives.

Down in the depths
Of the deep blue sea,
There's a sea serpent lurking
That you can't see.

This is not a serpent
That you should disregard.
He's three inches long
So be on your guard.

You'll See What I Mean

There goes Carl
Patrolling the crowd,
Quietly talking
To himself out loud.

Taking his time,
In sort of a hurry,
Concerned about something,
But he doesn't worry.

Not wanting to get
Where he wants to go,
Bidding farewell
By saying hello.

He tries to fit in
With tactics and schemes,
But the harder he tries
The stranger he seems.

There's something concerning
About Carl you see,
He isn't the sharpest
Bulb on the tree.

His elevator goes up
To the bottom floor,
And he isn't the brightest
Knife in the drawer.

Everyone he talks to
Knows the deal,
He's a few fries short
Of a Happy Meal.

Carl isn't typical
And he isn't routine,
Strike up a conversation,
You'll see what I mean.

Poor Millionaire

Poor and desperate millionaire
All alone and sitting there,
Gazing from an easy chair
With a blank and vacant sort of stare.

How it feels to be so rich,
Never had to dig a ditch,
Never suffered through employment—
A life of leisure and enjoyment.

All this money at your feet,
Only the finest food to eat.
Always granted every desire,
Clothed in the latest and greatest attire.

How provided for, you must feel,
Never had to beg or steal.
Filthy rich and what a deal,
Privilege has its own appeal.

And yet, you're lost without a friend
With way more money than you can spend.
No one ever calls your phone,
And so you sit there all alone.

No one here can help you now.
If only someone could, but how?
So unfortunate, such despair,
You poor and desperate millionaire.

Open Space

I constructed a humble home
That only has one wall.
It's ten feet long,
It's sturdy and strong,
And exactly eight feet tall.

Take a moment to look around
Because a moment is all it takes.
Just wait and see
And you'll agree
That I've made a few mistakes.

There's no space
For the fireplace
Because it wasn't in the master plan.

And I'm in here dealing
Without a ceiling
To mount the ceiling fan.

A basement here
Will not appear
Or an attic over my head.
And I couldn't begin to engineer
A location for the bed.

There's no hall,
There's only a wall,
There's no electrical power.
There's no call
For a sink at all,
There's not a bathroom or a shower.

And there's no roof
That's waterproof
To keep me warm and dry.
I can't contain
All that rain
From falling out of the sky.

And there's no way out
And there's no way in

So there's no need for any door.

And I wouldn't even

Know where to begin

To put the doorbell anymore.

And when I hear thunder

I sometimes wonder

Why I'm still living here.

Day after night,

No end in sight,

Fifty-two weeks a year.

There are no remedies

For these basic amenities,

But there's something about this place.

There's not a lot to it

When you review it

But there's plenty of open space.

A Toad and a Road

There he sat,
This courageous toad,
Waiting so patiently
By the side of the road.

Waiting for the moment
To cross the street.
Waiting to make
His journey complete.

His goal is to reach
To the other side,
As so many courageous
Toads have tried.

Could he be it,
Could he be the one
To accomplish the stunt
No toad's ever done?

With a full head of steam
And frantically hopping,
He crossed the highway
Without ever stopping.

Dodging the tires
That rolled his way,
Avoiding disaster,
Surviving the day.

Until one lone tire
From out of the blue,
At ninety miles an hour
Came barreling through.

And he took a hit,
Now he's flatter than flat,
And toads can't get
Much flatter than that.

He's stuck in a place
He'd rather not be,
Nailed by a tire
That he didn't see.

As flat as a dime,
Just another toad
Who picked the wrong time
To cross the road.

The Gift of Smell

Wash your feet and wash them well,
Wash them till they're clean.
Maybe it's your toes that smell
Down there in-between.

Wash them both and wash them often,
Wash them very well.
Because you may not be smelling
What everyone else can smell.

And anybody
with a nose
That has the
gift of smell
Could likely
come in contact
And not like it very well.

So wash those feet,
Then rinse and repeat
And omit that awful smell,
Your feet might smell okay to you
But everyone else can tell.

Twenty-Four Seven

The second-hand ticks,
The minute hand clicks,
And the clock keeps perfect pace.
I'd like to convert it
Or somehow divert it,
But that's simply not the case.

And there's no way to slow it,
Believe me, I know it,
The hand of time is true.
Time never slows
So onward it goes,
There's not a thing we can do.

It simply proceeds,
Twenty-four seven—
The clock will always chime.
Keeping the pace
For the human race
Time after time
after time.

IS THIS THING
EVEN WORKING?

Planet Mars

My family is moving
To planet Mars,
Which floats in the middle
Of a billion stars.

We're leaving our home
In Michigan soon,
The last part of May
Or the first part of June.

We've packed our luggage
And we're ready to go.
It'll take a long time
Because my dad drives slow.

We'll put up a house
On a nice piece of land,
Where the ocean spills water
All over the sand.

Where my mother plants flowers
On her hands and her knees,
And my father keeps busy
Trimming the trees.

There's so much to do
When we finally move in,
That we're not even sure
Even where to begin.

But we'll settle down
And when we do
It'll be a lot different
Than Kalamazoo.

And now we're counting
Our lucky stars
Because at last we're moving
To planet Mars.

The Catastrophic Flu

I need to paint my wretched house,
I can wait no more.
I need to add a coat of paint
From the ceiling to the floor.

And I need to paint it very soon,
One day this week will do.
A fresh coat of paint inside and out,
The perfect shade of blue.

But Thursday is no good for me
And Friday will not do.
Saturday I'll be coming down
With the catastrophic flu.

Sunday I'll be on the mend
And Monday, there's no way,
I was called for jury duty
So I'll be there all day.

Tuesday I'll see the doctor
From two o'clock till three,
I've got a bit of inflammation
That's bothering my knee.

Wednesday there's piano class
And then right after that,
I've got to haul the laundry
To the laundromat.

This leaves time for nothing else
With bedtime by eleven,
If only there were eight days now
Instead of only seven.

Walking Barefoot

Walking barefoot along the shore
I met a crab by the ocean floor
Who came within reach
Of my foot on the beach
Like no crab had before.

And that was precisely when
It opened a claw and then
Clamped down on my toe
And wouldn't let go
And I never walked barefoot again.

The Weekend

I woke up on Saturday morning—
The weekend was finally here!
There's a reason I get excited about it
Fifty-two times a year.

I can sit back and really relax,
Or I can do something exciting.
So I started out on the patio
With an hour's worth of writing.

After that, there was music to play
On a bona fide trombone.

I'm not very good at it yet—
Good thing I was alone!

The rest of the day I piddled around,
With nothing much to do.
I sat and watched the sun go down,
Admiring the view.

Sunday, I jumped in the lake for a swim,
The water was warm and inviting.
Then I caught a show
On the thirteenth row,
And that was rather exciting.

I returned to the house that night
After a weekend full of action,
Recalling all the fun that I had
And all the satisfaction.

I enjoyed everything that I did
And all the places I'd been,
Then Monday morning came back around
And spoiled the weekend again.

Shadow

Wherever I go,
Wherever I be,
My shadow is always
Standing by me.

We're always together
It never fails,
Down simple paths
And lonely trails.

Through times of joy
And bouts of sorrow,
Here today
And there tomorrow.

And when I'm facing
A typical day,
And my closest friends
Are miles away,

My shadow will always
Be standing by me
Wherever I go,
Wherever I be.

Unless of course
It's an overcast sky,
In which case
This wouldn't apply.

Opportunity Knocks

Opportunities are rare
And they're difficult to find,
So take one if you see one
If you're so inclined.

They can easily pass you by
If you're not paying attention,
Either because you're looking one way
Or stuck in another dimension.

And if you see one come along,
Don't let it disappear.
Opportunities can certainly vanish
As fast as they appear.

They don't simply hang around
As anyone can see,
Waiting for you to take your pick
Like apples from a tree.

Or sitting there like library books
Stacked upon the shelves,
Opportunities are hard to find
And seldom show themselves.

Sometimes they'll materialize
On any given day,
When they do, we usually manage
To let them slip away.

We need to seize the moment
Whenever the moment may strike,
Sometimes opportunities knock
But not as often as we'd like.

My Flying Submarine

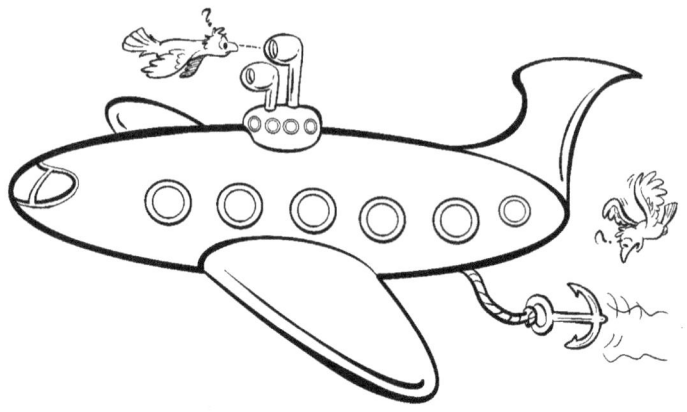

My flying submarine
Is an unusual machine—
A first in nautical aviation.
Two wings to glide it,
Some gadgets inside it,
It's a one-of-a-kind creation.

It can fly like a plane
Or soar like a bird—
It's a submarine in the sky.
It sails like a glider
With a pilot inside her,
It's an easy contraption to fly.

It can dart through the clouds
Above towering mountains
Or hover over terrain,
And the upkeep status
Of this apparatus
Is simple to maintain.

I should also mention
That this invention
Can do all of this and more.
So simple to conceive,
I still can't believe
Someone else didn't think of it before.

Stuck in the Mud

Can you believe it?
I'm stuck in the mud,
Surrounded by goop
And a bounty of crud.

I took a wrong step
Now look where I stand—
This isn't the day
I really had planned.

And I don't see anyone
That's anywhere near.
Isn't there anyone
At all around here?

Isn't there someone
Around I can find
Who maybe can help me
Get out of this bind?

Anchored in glop,
No means of escape,
Anyone can see
I'm in terrible shape.

Standing in slop
Up to my knees
Is a problem because
It's a hundred degrees!

And at a hundred degrees
There's a lot to lose,
Being stuck in the mud
Surrounded by ooze.

Look on the bright side
At least I won't freeze,
I'm as free as a bird
Down to my knees.

Summer School

Summer school for anyone
Should never be permitted,
So why is it required
That I should be admitted?

Just because I failed the courses
That I'm supposed to pass,
Is not a reason good enough
To send me back to class.

And it's not fair to drag me out
To a place I shouldn't be,
To study useless subject matter
That won't apply to me.

Because understanding science
Will never be my goal,
And I failed at economics
And history as a whole.

And geographic boundaries
Are indeed a handicap,
Because I can't find Australia
Or New Zealand on a map.

Nor did I grasp geometry
Where dimensions were concerned.
I failed to master the many lessons
Perhaps I should have learned.

So off to school I go again
To the place that I deplore,
And attempt to pass
Every single class
That I failed the time before.

To me, this type of punishment
Seems mercilessly cruel.
Not even the janitor spends this much time
Hanging out at school.

Artificial Intelligence

When we surrender our usefulness
And AI takes control,
We won't stand the slightest chance
With technology on patrol.

It's going to overcome us all,
There's no way around it.
If there's a safeguard to install,
No one's ever found it.

Artificial intelligence is here to stay—
It's not going anywhere!
And in no time, it'll rule the day
And govern the whole affair.

AI is here for the long haul,
It's not going to wait.
By the time we comprehend it all,
It's going to be too late.

This will be our entire demise
When the takeover is complete.
We better be able to adapt—otherwise,
We'll all be obsolete!

I don't agree with it, of course,
And I'll say, one thing more:
When AI becomes the dominant force,
They won't need us anymore.

My Doughnut

My brother ate my doughnut
On the table over there.
He knows exactly how to eat it
But doesn't know how to share.

He knows it's not the thing to do,
He knows it isn't fair.
He knows he's now in trouble,
But he really doesn't care.

Never thought that he would do it,
Didn't think that he would dare.
Now I think he'll eat my doughnuts
Anytime or anywhere.

And since he ate my doughnut
On the table over there,
I ate the doughnut meant for him,
Just to make it fair.

If Nature Would Allow

Ever notice when it snows
It's always freezing cold?
I know the scene is quite serene,
And something to behold.

But wouldn't it be interesting
If perhaps somehow,
It could snow during summertime
If nature would allow?

Then we wouldn't have to tremble
And we certainly wouldn't quiver.

We could still enjoy the snow,
And we wouldn't have to shiver.

We wouldn't have to plow the streets,
Or hunker down inside.
We could walk along the sidewalk,
And never slip and slide.

Wouldn't it be miraculous
If it snowed but didn't freeze?
If only it would snow sometimes
At ninety-five degrees.

A Ton of Bricks

There I was minding my business
Under a ton of bricks,
Next to stacks of empty buckets
And sacks of mortar mix.

There was no one around to tell me
That I shouldn't be standing there.
If there's a sign forbidding it,
I didn't see it anywhere.

Suddenly, out of nowhere
The bricks came crashing down.
Who would've thought this could happen
In this quiet little town?

And all those heavy bricks
Landed right upon my head.
It would have been better
Had they landed somewhere else instead!

And I would've moved aside in time
Had I the wherewithal,
But it hit me like a ton of bricks,
And that's the last thing I recall.

Elbow Room

I only eat the finest garbage
Available to me,
Like the French are with the wine they drink
And the English with their tea.

Sifting through the rubbish
At an undisclosed location,
It's pointless to prolong
This mouth-watering temptation.

I am quite particular
About the garbage I consume,
So I need a perfect garbage can
And a lot of elbow room.

Dinner time is fast approaching
And I can hardly wait—
I go after garbage
Like a fish goes after bait.

I don't drive a Lamborghini
Or dress the latest fashion.
You can see
That garbage to me
Is my only passion.

I may be truly destitute,
I may be empty handed,
But I'm wealthy in my garbage choice,
If I can be so candid.

I possess no true integrity—
A reputation I have earned.
But I hold the highest standards
Where garbage is concerned.

Once He Was Clever

He has a brain
That he never uses—
When he tries to think,
It only confuses.

He studied and studied
Book after book,
He did what he had to—
Whatever it took.

He earned his diploma
But then after school,
He didn't use
His brain as a tool.

He tucked away genius
But forgot where he hid it.
He didn't realize,
Whenever he did it,

That he would require
His brain every day
To think clever thoughts
And of things to say.

And now that he needs it
There's no brain to be found.
He searched through his memory
And looked all around.

But he found it not,
His search was in vain.
Oh how he wishes
He could locate his brain.

Because he needs to think
A lot more than most,
He's smart as a whip
But dumb as a post.

It looks like his brain
Is gone forever,
And now he's befuddled
Where once he was clever.

Pot of Potatoes

On top of the stove
After laborious toil,
A pot of potatoes
Comes to a boil.

Not big on flavor
Mediocre and flat,
But it fills up the belly
To make up for that.

And you won't be alarmed
At the price on the tag,
You pay a few dollars
For a two-pound bag.

They're not too appealing
And not too desired,
But if you're hungry
That's all that's required.

I added some salt
And butter to taste,
So all those potatoes
Don't go to waste.

And I ate so many
I can't eat anymore,
That's what potatoes
Are actually for.

Potatoes are as bland
As potatoes can be,
But you'd eat one too,
If you were as hungry as me.

When I Was Eighteen

I was eighteen one day,
Then eighty the next.
I stand here bewildered
And a little perplexed.

Because there was eighteen
In front of my face,
And suddenly it vanished
Without a trace.

And now that I'm old
And over the hill,
I curse my dilemma
And live by the pill.

I frequent the doctor,
The pharmacy too,
Embarrassing, yes—
What else can I do?

I don't have the balance
I had years ago,
And my memory is gone
That much I know.

I walk with the aid
Of a cane in my hand,
I've had all the aging
I think I can stand.

The aches and the pains
Are too many to list.
When I was eighteen,
This didn't exist.

How come it's not
Like it was back then?
Oh how I wish
I was eighteen again.

In All Actuality

He thought he'd climb
An uncharted hill
Completely on his own—
Turned out to be
The smallest mountain
The world has ever known.

Here Lies the King

Here lies the king
That ruled the lands
With a hasty temper
And greedy hands.

Shields of armor
And swords of steel
And lowly peasants
Required to kneel.

Superior soldiers
For stark defense
Made all the difference
And it made good sense.

Castle walls
From roof to floor;
Archers guarded
The castle door.

Dungeon chambers
Of stone and mortar;
Prisoners there
Received no quarter.

Taxes levied
To fit his needs;
Lawlessness
And awful deeds.

Collecting gold
By hook or crook,
And keeping the most
Of what he took.

No one dared
Defy the king,
No one did
That sort of thing.

He called the shots
As he saw fit,
He made the rules
And that was it.

Now here he lies
No land to rule,
No lowly servant,
No bumbling fool.

For years he reigned
From land to sea,
But another day
Will never be.

In his presence
One had to bow,
But no one has
To do it now.

Being the ruler
Might sound great,
But even the king
Must meet his fate.

No Horsing Around

Out in a field
I spotted a sight,
A horse doing tricks
For his own delight.

Jumping around
And prancing in place,
Sort of a silly
Kind of look on his face.

He bucked for a while,
Pretending to be
A rodeo horse
In some jamboree.

But he wasn't finished
So he didn't stop there,
He leaped from the ground
And twirled through the air.

He spun around backward
In a circular motion,
Causing all kinds
Of crazy commotion.

He stood on one leg
Just balancing there,
Like an acrobat does
At the county fair.

If my friends could see this,
They couldn't conceive it.
I wanted to tell them,
But they wouldn't believe it.

Then the horse caught me looking
And halted, of course,
Then started acting
More like a horse.

Grunting and snorting
And picking through hay,
Flicking his tail
In the usual way.

Nothing elaborate
Nothing to see,
Me watching him
Him watching me.

Standing there staring
Four hooves on the ground,
Nothing too special
No horsing around.

A Job Well Done

You do what you must
When it must be done,
It can be unpleasant
And not much fun.

But it must be done
When the situation requires,
Either with brains
Or a good set of pliers.

So you tackle the job
With plain determination,
With easy mathematics
And basic calculation.

And when it's complete
And done is the job,
And the doohickey aligns
With the thingamabob,

And all the pieces
Fall into place,
But you double-check it
Just in case,

And you catch your breath
Because the job is through,
And you do nothing more
For there's nothing to do.

Then you can simply
Sit back and admire,
A job well done
That will only inspire.

But it can be unpleasant
And not much fun,
But you do what you must
When it must be done.

Chalkboards

Chalkboards are history
And this is a fact,
Like the abacus we used
To add and subtract.

Chalkboards are ancient
Like the shag carpet floor,
Like the polyester shirt
I don't wear anymore.

And we don't need chalk
Because we don't have boards,
And erasers are outdated
Like those Model T Fords.

And they're seldom seen
At all anymore,
Because teachers don't use them
Like they used them before.

You won't find one
On a classroom wall,
Because no one can locate
A chalkboard at all.

They either went extinct
A long time ago,
Or our stockpile of slate
Is critically low.

Music Is for Everyone

Music has a certain flavor
It has a certain groove,
It makes a person swing and sway,
It makes a body move.

Music makes you stomp your feet,
It makes you clap your hands,
There's something cool about it
Everybody understands.

It forces you to keep the rhythm
And maybe sing along,
It puts a bunch of notes together
Right where they belong.

It's clearly indiscriminate
It electrifies the soul.
Music is what makes the youth
Completely lose control.

It motivates the family
To dance across the floor.
If your parents once were sitting down,
They won't be anymore.

It nourishes your conscience,
It stimulates the core.
Music seems to fill a void,
Like nothing has before.

Throughout the very best of times,
Yesterday included,
Music is for everyone
And no one is excluded.

And throughout the hardest times
It understands your sorrow,
Music does the same today
As it will do tomorrow.

Pillow of Stone

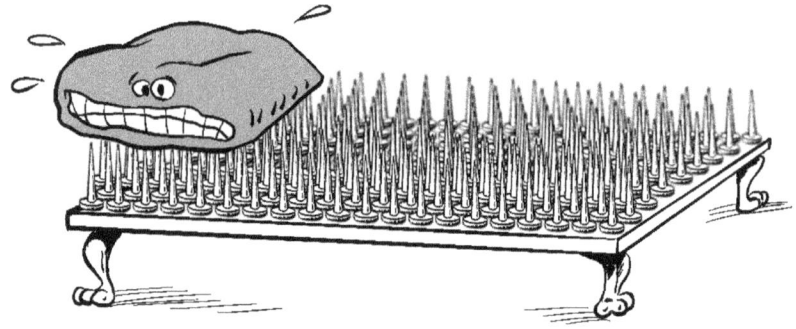

When I go to sleep
I'm always alone,
On a bed of nails
And pillow of stone.

And a bed of nails
Only pokes to the bone,
And my head isn't bothered
By a pillow of stone.

I'm quite comfortable
With my head on a rock.
I go to bed at ten,
And get up at six o'clock.

But my cat will not join me.
She has her suspicions.
Perhaps, she's not used
To these cozy conditions.

My bed's made of steel.
It's sturdy and strong,
But she sleeps on the couch
Where she doesn't belong.

She goes after butterflies,
And pounces on frogs
She leaps after lizards,
And hides from the dogs.

She plays like a kitten
With the string on my shoe,
And does everything else
Like a cat would do.

But still, she won't join me,
So I'm always alone,
And the reason behind this
May never be known.

Believe Me, I Just Lied

Whenever you look to find me
And you don't see me there,
Simply turn around and then
Give the room a stare.

You'll find me in the corner
So look in that direction,
I generally quarantine over there
In an isolated section.

I do not socialize in the center
And I don't mingle on the side,
If I told you I'd be hanging there
Then, believe me, I just lied.

You won't find me in a crowd
Nor in a congregation—
It's too distressing and way too loud
And it causes agitation.

So I took the places I used to go
And put them all behind me,
Now over in the corner
Is exactly where you'll find me.

Don't go looking for me
In some overpopulated section,
You'll find me in the corner
So look in that direction.

Anything You Can Do

Here in my classroom,
Here at my school,
There sits a student
Who isn't a fool.

Sitting beside me,
Acquiring knowledge—
Too smart for books,
Too smart for college.

His test results show
An incredible score.
He knows all there is,
Plus a little bit more.

He has all the answers,
He studies the clues.
He fathoms curriculum
Like yesterday's news.

They say he possesses
No tricks or gimmicks.
He unravels the answer
With plain academics.

There is no subject
He knows nothing about.
There isn't a formula
He can't figure out.

Electrons and atoms
And neutrons and such,
He understands all of it
A little too much.

He tackles equations
That no one can do—
He could show Einstein
A theory or two.

His English is perfect
Right down to the letter,
Anything you can do
He can do better.

He needs no assistance,
No tutor required.
His brain has a current
That's perfectly wired.

He never failed a test,
He never flunked a quiz.
I wish I had a brain
That functioned like his.

He's mastered science
And calculus too.
He's smarter than me,
He's smarter than you.

Be it physics or geometry
Or history or spelling,
How smart will he get?
There's really no telling.

A PhD
Wouldn't be so tough,
And a master's degree
Would be simple enough.

Whatever the study,
Whatever the test,
He knows the answers
And he knows them best.

Of course he's brilliant
Between the ears,
He's taken these classes
For ninety-five years.

I've Got a Hunch

There's a rumor out there
But I think it's true,
And I've got a hunch
About what to do.

It's a feeling I get
At least once a day,
It's a feeling I get
When I'm feeling this way.

It's an obvious curse
And I'll verify,
The feeling gets worse
As time goes by.

There's a rumor out there
And I've got a hunch,
That yes, once again,
It's time for lunch!

The Earth Today

The Earth today
Has something to say:
"Why must you people
Treat me this way?

Must you contaminate
All that I give?
And make it unbearable
For everyone to live?

You poison my land
And my water supply.
You send all your smoke
Into the sky.

So many chemicals
Now fill the air,
There isn't much room
For oxygen there.

You've tainted my mountains
In toxic debris,
Can you not tell
What it's doing to me?

You bury your garbage
Deep in my belly,
It's not very nice—
It's nasty and smelly!

And the oceans, so littered
With noxious waste,
That the fish have forgotten
How the ocean should taste.

If you keep this up
Over land and shore,
This place won't be fit
To inhabit anymore.

It's out of my hands
And that's why I say,
Why must you people
Treat me this way?"

Here Stands a Chair

Here stands a chair
In need of repair.
It's there on the floor,
No good anymore.

Nobody wants it,
Nobody cares,
No one's concerned
About any repairs.

It stands alone
With nothing around,
Not doing a thing,
Not making a sound.

Gathering cobwebs,
The obligatory dust,
Years of neglect
And decades of rust.

So it's falling apart,
It's as simple as that.
It used to seat people
Whenever they sat.

It was strong long ago
But not anymore.
If you sit in it now,
You'll land on the floor.

But it stands where it sits
And it sits where it stands,
It's one of those infamous
And offbeat brands.

It's in such a state
Of complete disrepair,
That it might be too late
To save this chair.

For it's only a chair
There on the floor.
No good to anyone,
Not anymore.

Slim to None

Want to win the lottery?
I think anybody would.
I would like to match the numbers
Someday if I could.

Pick some numbers here and there
Scribble them on the card,
Buy a ticket anywhere—
That part isn't hard.

You could win a billion dollars,
Maybe even more.
That would be a lot more money
Than you've ever had before.

And spend the money as you wish,
There's nothing you can't buy.
You'll have more than you'll ever need
And that should satisfy.

But always remember that gambling
Is not for everyone.
You have the chance to win it all
But the odds are slim to none.

Bluebird

It's freezing outside
This time of year,
So what would a bluebird
Be doing out here?

There's snow on the window,
There's ice on the ground.
If I were a bluebird,
I would not hang around.

The wind is relentless,
There's nowhere to hide.
And only a polar bear
Would step outside.

There's nothing to drink,
There's nothing to eat.
And he doesn't have
Any shoes on his feet.

And the sun today
Can nowhere be seen.
Just step outside,
You'll see what I mean.

Yet, the bluebird remains
Covered in frost.
Maybe he's stupid,
Maybe he's lost.

I wouldn't be here
If I was a bird.
Haven't I told you—
Haven't you heard?

What would a bluebird
Be doing out here?
It's freezing outside
This time of year.

My Innocent Nose

Your shoes smell bad
And they certainly stink,
You need to wash them
That's what I think!

The stench is that
Of some fish filets,
Left outside
For thirteen days.

The scent can bring
A man to tears,
Who hasn't cried
In twenty years.

An aroma worse
Than stagnate air,
Much too foul
For one to bear.

Like rotten eggs
That were never sold,
Out of date
And three months old.

Garbage stinks
And it can be gross,
But even that
Isn't even close.

My innocent nose
And my watering eyes
Long for me
To hear their cries.

I better leave
And get out fast.
This can't go on—
This cannot last!

Open the window
Or open the door,
The scent is worse
Than it was before.

You ran off the dog
And scared the cat,
It's hard to believe
Your shoes did that.

I caught my breath,
I cleared my eyes,
And found out much
To my surprise,

I see exactly
Why they smell so strong,
Those shoes were my shoes
All along!

Catch

When learning to catch
The best place to start
Is right in your own backyard.

Catching the ball
Is the easy part—
It's hanging on that's hard.

Don't Read a Book

Do you realize what happens
When you read a book?
First, you'll have to open it,
Then you'll have to look.

It's all written down,
There's nothing you need.
All you have to do,
Is learn how to read.

And once you start reading
You can't put it down—
You'll be obsessed
By the verb and the noun.

And you'll be satisfied,
Page after page—
Reading is beneficial
At any old age.

Grasp what the author
Is trying to tell.
It's all so revealing,
And it's all very well.

Start with Aesop's fables,
Read some Edger Allen Poe,
Or pursue some other authors
That you didn't even know.

Check out Samuel Clemens,
Get loose with Dr. Seuss,
Or go from William Shakespeare
Up to Mother Goose.

If short stories interest you,
Charles Dickens comes to mind.
Oh, the plots that you'll uncover—
The conclusions you will find.

Whether it's the truth
Or whether it's fiction,
You can find a library
In any jurisdiction.

It's a book, that's all—
It's material to read.
It's all black and white,
It's something we need.

Now open it up
Then take a look,
And see what you're missing
When you don't read a book.

About Mark J. Beasley

By the age of sixteen, Mark Beasley was writing and cataloging the first drafts of what would become a lifelong endeavor. His first book, *It's Me, That's Who!*, became a reality when a friend introduced him to illustrator, Kem Welch. Their ongoing collaboration makes for steady progress and encourages Mark to write more.

As a lifelong resident of Charleston, South Carolina, Mark enjoys motorcycle rides through the Lowcountry. He occasionally plays bass guitar and sings backup as well. Mark has one brother who lives out of state and several first cousins in Charleston and upstate South Carolina who he spends time with. He also enjoys socializing with close friends.

.

www.ingramcontent.com/pod-product-compliance
Lightning Source LLC
Chambersburg PA
CBHW051145120626
46547CB00012B/946